Waves of life

Rajshree Shikkewal

BookLeaf Publishing

India | USA | UK

Presentation by *BookLeaf Publishing*

Web: www.bookleafpub.com

E-mail: info@bookleafpub.com

ISBN: 9789363315129

First edition 2024

To my mom (1959-2023),

I am eternally grateful to you.

You continue to inspire me every day,

May you be happy wherever you are…

When I met her

I met her after a very long time,
Her face had wrinkles,
She didn't recognise me,
For I was someone who used to believe in the
beauty of dreams,
And she did not know anymore what dreams are,
I went to her and introduced myself,
Finally, she remembered me,
I asked her
'What have you done all these years'?
'What happened to the best moments of your
life'?
'Did you really live your life the way you
wanted'?

She said, 'You are still a kid who hasn't
experienced the world yet'.
She smiled and turned away,
Mirror did not allow me to hug her.

HER

Do you see that pair of baggy eyes,
And how gracefully her lips curl when she
smiles,
Do you realise how deeply she cuts herself with
the shards of her own words,
Every time when she utters the words 'I am
fine'...

Irony

Why does everything happen all at once or
nothing move at all in life,
You are either in the limelight or in the darkness,
You are either all over the place or lost in
nothingness,
You are either relaxing at the shore or off-track
in the sea like a ship without a compass,
You are either a garden in full bloom or a barren
land craving for rain,
You either long for a companion to share your
journey or love your solitude,
You want either to win over the whole world or
lose yourself,
You feel either too many emotions at once or go
numb,
Perhaps these are the ironies of being human!

Spring would never be same

There would be spring again this year,
It will bring back colours and blossoms,
Summer, rain, fall and winter would follow,
The cycle of seasons will continue,

There would be daybreak again tomorrow,
It will bring back sunshine and smiles,
Afternoon, evening and night would follow,
The cycle of days and nights will continue,

I too would continue with my chores,
Growing a day older with each passing day,
Sometimes I'd smile,
Sometimes I'd cry,
And every moment I'd be missing you, Mom,
The journey of my life will continue,
But the spring would never be the same again.

Drown

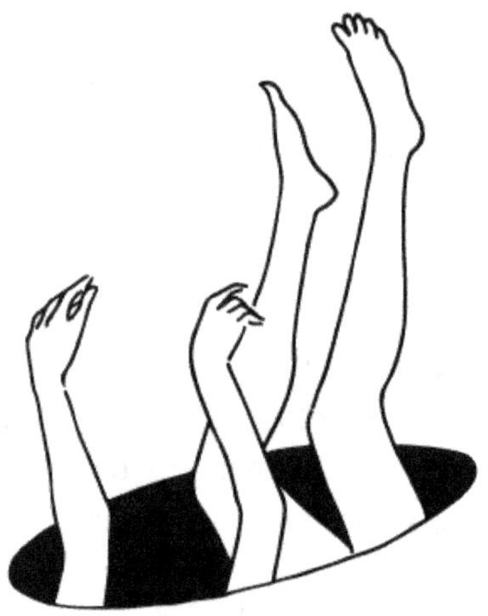

Now I see the end of summer,
It's June, and it has started raining,
Dark clouds loom over,
Life goes cold,

Raindrops hit my window panes,
Trees, flowers and pavements are washed out,
The world looks like a muddy puddle,

Some lives drown in the gloomy weather,
Like a helpless child getting drenched in the
rain,
Craving for shelter and losing hope to see the
sunshine ever again.

Waves of life

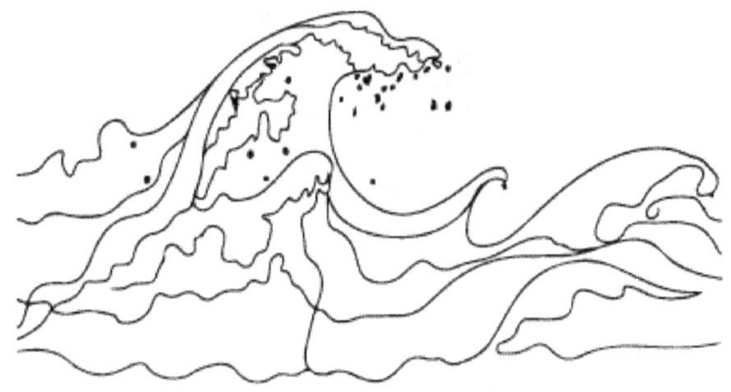

Life hits you in waves,
Sometimes gentle,
Sometimes hard, especially when you least
expect it,
It does not give you time to slow down,

Days are like struggles to keep ourselves from
drowning,
We accept life's agonies,
And go through the cycle of sufferings,
Where happiness seems like a long-lost dream.

Dreams are not real

Dreams are surreal,
They lure you into believing something that's
nowhere close to real,

Beware, dreams are traps,
Open your eyes and look around,
After all, life isn't a bed of roses as it may seem,

Wake up, dreams are deceitful,
What may seem to last forever,
Comes crashing down in seconds,

No more lies,
No more games,
No stardust is going to touch and transit you to
the other side of reality,

Some people say that life is nothing without
dreams,
But we ought to remember that life just goes on,
And dreams are not real!

Chasing the light

I wandered and roamed,
Rode up the hill,
And crossed the bridge leading to the other side
of the road,
I took the path to a lesser-known place,
Then there was a pause...
Was it my destination?
No...
I turned back and decided to follow the light,
I took the path with twists and turns,
Filled with unknown,
I was chasing the light of the setting sun.

What do I feel

I do not know what I feel today,
Or perhaps I know too much,
But what I fear the most is being seen feeling
anything,
It will strip me,
And leave me vulnerable,

Wrapped in the blanket of emotions,
I lie down on the bed of sadness,
Resting my head on the pillow of heartaches,
Mourning with the silence of the night.

Homesick

People say they want to relive their childhood,
But I don't want to,
I was so naive,
I believed that
...dreams come true,
...somebody would always have your back,
...and we get to choose our paths,

Nobody prepares you for adulthood,
Nobody teaches lessons like
...dreams are far beyond the walls of reality,
...you have to be strong enough not to fall,
...and even if you fall, you will have to get up on
your own,
...the memories you create would merely be a
graveyard of nostalgia to spend your lonely
nights,
...still, you will constantly feel homesick for a
place that might not even exist.

October

The blazing leaf bids adieu to the tree it had held
onto for so long,
It falls on earth in silence like a teardrop from
the eye,
And gazes at the clear blue sky,
Waiting for the crisp winter breeze to carry it
along to a new destination,
It accepts inevitable fate and trusts its new
companion like it's going to lead it to salvation,
And the tree stands still...
Feeling like it has lost something precious,
Helplessly caught in a cycle vicious,
And I ponder...
Would the tree cherish the same bond with a
new leaf,
Would it ever find relief,
Would it miss the old leaf's amber,
The way I am going to miss you and our time
together in October.

Twists of Destiny

Too close to saying goodbye,
Too far to be together,
Distances between us,
Still remains,

Too strong to break,
Too fragile to be inviolable,
Somehow this bond,
Still remains,

Too surreal to be real,
Too real to be delusive,
Unfulfilled dream,
Still remains,

Too intricate to discern,
Too simple to be perplexing,
Unsolved mystery,
Still remains.

My favourite story

The nights have thousands of stories to tell,
But my favourite stories are about you,
When we used to take the road less travelled,
Playing the forgotten songs,
Looking at the distant city lights,
And reaching the unexplored destinations,

The stories still remind me that it's the company
that makes a journey more beautiful,

Silent language of tears

In the light of the Crescent moon,
Savouring the silence,
Beneath the golden tree she stood,
Benighted she was,
Bereaved she was,
For she lost her loved one,
And was left all alone,
Same was the place where they
once met,
Same was the place where they once embraced,
They were oppressed,
They were rejected,
Profane they turned,
For they wished to be united for eternity,
But destiny had other plans,
He left for his heavenly abode,
Leaving her to collect the reminiscences,

Sailing down the sea of emotions,
Wind caressing her hair,
To decipher the silent language of tears,
Her only companion was despair.

Dear Traveller

My dear fellow traveller,
Together we have stepped on new soils,
To listen to the forgotten songs and stories,
Together we have walked miles,

With the air filled with chirps and bliss,
Tumult of our mundane days cease,
With the sun bidding adios,
The beauty of crimson skies our eyes could
seize,

We pack our bags and start heading towards our
homes,
Leaving with the memories of new paths
unravelled,
But do not ask me where I come from,
For my home is every place I have travelled.

Numb

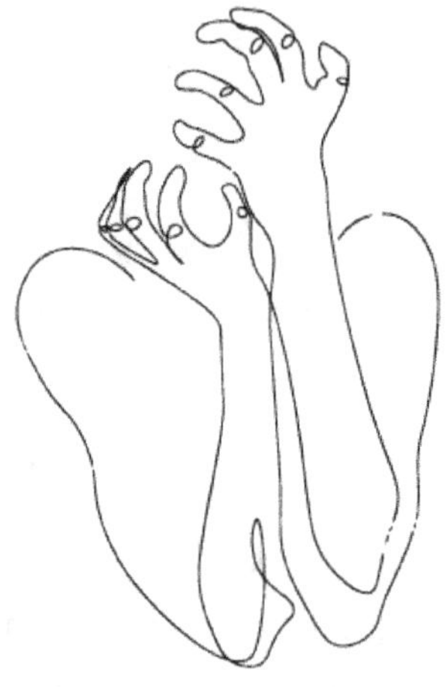

There is darkness...
In a moment I turn stone cold,
Teary eyes and a lump in my throat

There is an indecipherable emptiness
There is turmoil and chaos in my mind,
It makes me numb,
The only emotion I feel is,
Sands of time slipping from my hand.

Incomplete Poetries

There is something poetic about those
unfulfilled dreams,
Something beautiful as it seems,

Untravelled places,
Unread books,
Unsaid words,
Unexpressed emotions,
Sleepless nights,
And in the mind goes on and on a series of
endless fights,

Canvas left half painted,
Broken pieces of self that remain unmended,
Lump in the throat,
Tears welled up in the eyes,

Unachieved goals,
Unaccompanied journeys,
Unacceptable guilts,
Unrequited love,
Undesirable pains,

There is something poetic about those
unfulfilled dreams,
Something beautiful as it seems,
About unsolved mysteries,
Unwritten stories,
And incomplete poetries...

FREE

When I left my body,
I knew I would drift away in the tunnel of light,
But I waited to have a look at my body,
And introspect about my days spent living with
it,
I could see the wounds,
But felt no pain,
Though feeling light,
It was heavy that all my efforts had gone in vain,

Pleasing others,
Seeking their approval,
I lived each day as per their wishes,
I had killed my own desires,
I had no dreams left,

Now I was free,
Enlightened by the wisdom,
Worldly pleasures are superficial!

BITTER TRUTH

Yes! it's true,
People leave when adversity strikes,
When at low,
That's when no one stands beside,

Yes! it's true,
The promises made are verbal traps,
Those are illusions created to temporarily fill the
gaps,

Yes! it's true,
The pretentious are respected,
And the natural ones simply get rejected,

Yes! it's true,
The age of downfall is here,
When the bitter truths die,
And lies survive.

DON'T JUDGE!!!

You haven't walked the roads I have,
You haven't fallen down at the places I have,
You haven't fought the battles I have,
You haven't even seen those wounds I had
suffered,
You don't know how I got those scars,
You haven't walked into my shoes,
You haven't sunk down to the bottom from
where I rose up,
You haven't learnt the lessons I have,
You were not fortunate enough to have
experienced what I have,
DON'T JUDGE ME!!!

Crossroads of Life...

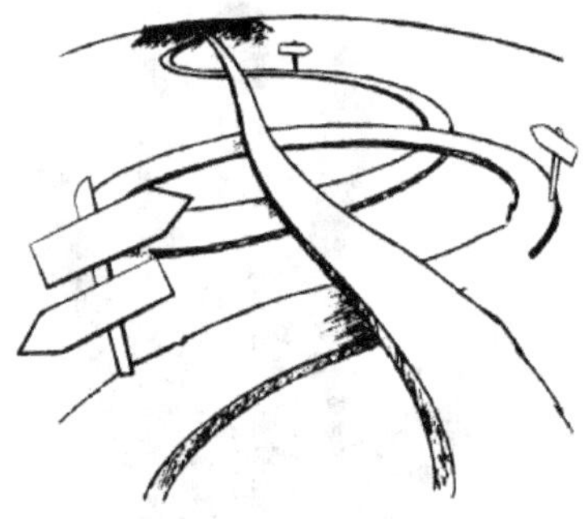

Some moments just fly,
And mind cannot decipher,
Whether those are priceless memories,
Or the things one should forget,
If those were the happy days,
How can those memories make eyes wet,

There are tangled thoughts,
We stand at the crossroads of choices,
Trying to figure out which path to take,
Whether the result would be victory,
Or it would be one more mistake,

Some of the doors are slammed in face,
Mind gets clouded,
It feels wearied,
Dreams get shrouded,

Though for the time being,
It remains undiscerned,
In the end,
Life would be a treasure of lessons learned!

Shadows!

Yes, we promised to be together,
And shared our emotions,
Then why are we separated today,
By the walls of silence,
And the walls of darkness,
When we know it's difficult to stay apart,
Why do these walls exist,

It takes a lot to smile,
When the emotional turmoil refuses to settle
down,
Soul gets tired,
And heart feels broken,

Shadows hide the light of love,
But every dark night has a shining dawn,
Tears too will run dry,
Heart will be waiting to see the sunshine!

DISSOLVE IN THE RAIN!

The clouds gathered,
And greyed out the blue sky,
Slowly I saw the small droplets falling on the
leaves,
On the ground.

Rain settled the dust,
And washed out the road,
Looked like the colours of nature were flowing.

And I felt like standing out there,
Savouring solitude,
And soaking those drops,
Wish I were made up of mud,
So that I could get dissolved in the rain,
And disappear from the world,
To be one with the earth.

The Caged Soul

The treacherous plans of destiny,
Take a toll on the soul sometimes,
With the dark clouds hovering over the skies of
ambitions,
Vision gets blurred with the dust of an unending
storm,
Desires seem to be caged in the memories of
past,

Running in the howling wilderness,
It's the time when the voice inside starts
screaming for freedom,

Freedom from anger and disaffection,
From grief and resentment,
From the pain deep down that pulls the self
down,
And drags to the trough of despair...

After a while

After a while,
Caterpillar breaks free from cocoon,
Turning into a beautiful butterfly,
Unconfined, unbound,
Spreading its wings,
Becoming the master of it's fate,

After a while,
She breaks free from her shell,
Rising elegantly with fortitude and indomitable
spirit,
Taking into her own hands,
The power to transform her own destiny.

Warm winter

The fall is over,
Do you feel cold when you touch the
windowpane,
Do you feel chilly & crisp breezes,
Here comes the winter again!

It's the time...
...for conversations over hot coffee,
...to express feelings once left unsaid,
...to wrap up precious moments & move to a
new year,

It's the time...
...to reflect and introspect our deeds,
...to light up a path for the ones who have lost
hope,
...to let go of the grudges that we hold,

The year ends with festivities,
It's an opportunity to make the winter warm,
As we embark on a journey again
With miles to go on!